ROMANS!

MOIRA BUTTERFIELD

FRANKLIN WATTS
LONDON•SYDNEY

Weird True Facts! the boring stuff...

This edition published 2014 by Franklin Watts

Copyright © Franklin Watts 2014
Franklin Watts
338 Euston Road
London NW1 3BH

Franklin Watts Australia
Level 17/207 Kent Street
Sydney, NSW 2000

A CIP catalogue record for this book
is available from the British Library.

Dewey no: 937

ISBN: 978 1 4451 2969 3

Printed in China

Franklin Watts is a division of Hachette Children's Books, an Hachette UK company

www.hachette.co.uk

Series editor: Sarah Ridley
Editor in Chief: John C. Miles
Designer: www.rawshock.co.uk/Jason Anscomb
Art director: Jonathan Hair
Picture research: Diana Morris
Artwork: Lee Montgomery

Picture credits: Algol/Shutterstock: 22t. Alinari Archives/Corbis: 6b. andersphoto/
Shutterstock: 9br. Anirudh's Magic Eye/Shutterstock: 26b. Arly/Shutterstock: 25tr.
Art Gallery Collection/Alamy: 13tl. Zvonimir Atletic/Shutterstock: 7b. Nina B/
Shutterstock: 25cl. Martin Bache/Alamy: 20t. Alessandra Benedetti/Corbis: 23t.
Bettmann/Corbis: 15t, 26t. Alexey Biryukov/Shutterstock: front cover bc.
Brasil2/istockphoto: 24cr. Butha/Shutterstock: 12bl.Dagli Orti/Art Archiv/Alamy: 14br.
Gianni Dagli Orti/Art Archive/Alamy: 14c, 16b. De Agostini/Getty Images: 16t.
Araldo de Luca/Corbis: 21b. Mary Evans PL: front cover br, 14bl, 15c, 28b.
Mary Evans PL/Alamy: 29b. Franklin Watts: 10b. Luigi Galante/DK Images: 19.
Heritage Images/Corbis:18. imagestalk/Shutterstock: front cover cr.
Interfoto/Alamy: 24br. Interfoto/Sammlung Rauch/Mary Evans PL: 17tl.
Javarman/Shutterstock: front cover tl, front cover tr. Mimmo Jodice/Corbis: 17tr.
Anna Khomub/Shutterstock: 29tc. Veniamin Kraskov/Shutterstock: 28tl.
Alain Lauga/Shutterstock: 17b. Lebrecht/Alamy: 8t, 27t. Makc/Shutterstock:
02-02, 04-05, 30-31. mountainpix/Shutterstock: 7t, 13b. Museum of London: 20b.
NGIC/Alamy: 10t. North Wind Pictures/Alamy: 23b. Paul Pantazescu/istockphoto:
02-03, 04-05. Regien Paassen/Shutterstock: front cover cl. Bill Perry/Shutterstock:6t.
PerseoMedusa/Shutterstock: 9l. Mauro Pezzotta /Shutterstock: 12b.
Photos12/Alamy: 8b. Radist/Dreamstime: 24cl. Raluktudor/Dreamstime: 24bl.
Route 66/Shutterstock: 27b. Fabrizio Ruggeri/Alamy: 12t. Schankz/Shutterstock: 17t.
Skryl/Shutterstock: 29tl. Alexander A Sobolev/Shutterstock: 02-03, 04-05, 30-31.
Frederick Soltan/Corbis: 28tr. Damir Spanic/istockphoto: 11b. Stapleton Collection/BAL: 11t. Robert
Szakiel/istockphoto: 28c. Gari Wyn Williams/Alamy: 13tr. Roger Wood/Corbis: 21t.

Every attempt has been made to clear copyright. Should there be any inadvertent omission
please apply to the publisher for rectification.

ROMANS!

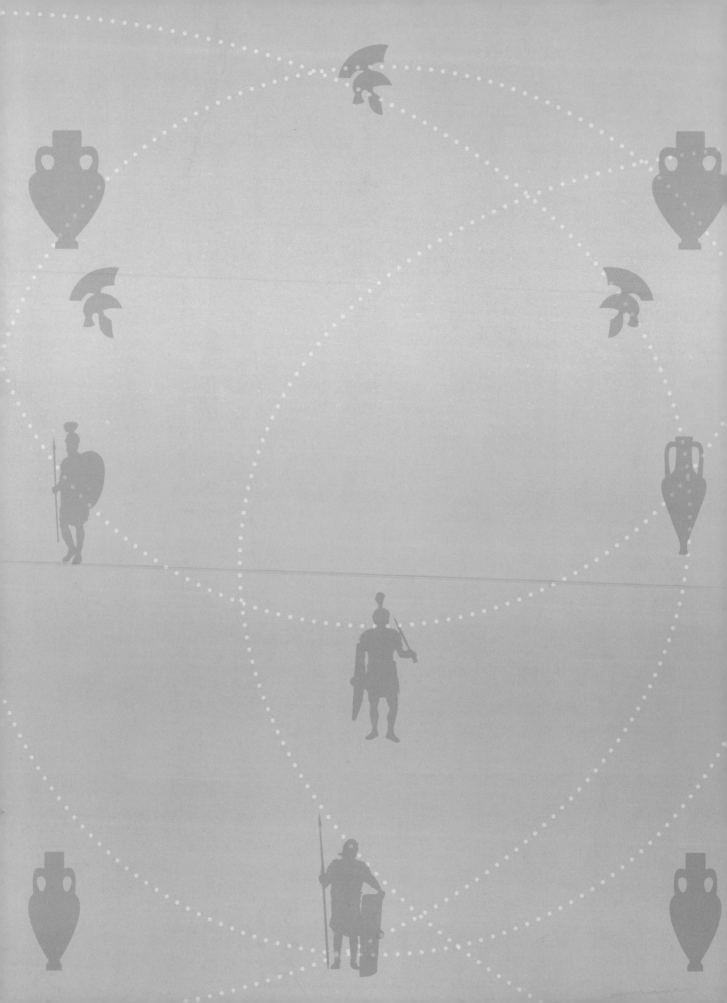

CONTENTS

Gods, geese and Gauls — Rome begins   6

Who's in charge? — Posh plotters and rowdy rebels   8

Brilliant bullies — Don't argue with the army   10

Ranking Romans — Who's up and who's down   12

Murderers and madmen — Shocking celebrity stories   14

Life the Roman way — Births, marriages and deaths   16

Home in Rome — The Empire indoors   18

Get by at the baths — Looking good, Latin-style   20

Fish porridge, anyone? — Food fit for an empire   22

A trip to the temple — Be nice to the gods, or else!   24

See the show — Mind the blood   26

Party! — Celebrate Roman-style   28

Glossary and websites   30

Index   32

ROME BEGINS

The ancient Roman Empire began in the area we now call Italy. In time the Romans came to rule over many parts of Europe and North Africa. Here's how it all began.

WHY IS YOUR MUM SO HAIRY?

Legend says that a Trojan prince called Aeneas sailed to Italy to found a new land. His descendants were baby twins called Romulus and Remus, whose father was Mars, the god of war. An evil uncle put the twins into a basket and threw them into the River Tiber, but the babies were rescued and fed by a she-wolf.

As adults the twins decided to build their own city but couldn't agree where it should be, so in 75 BCE Romulus murdered Remus, built the city where he wanted it and called it Rome. To accept this story, you need to believe that babies can have a god for a dad and a she-wolf for a mum. In reality it's just a myth.

A Roman statue showing Romulus and Remus with their wolf mother.

Nobody knows what was in the sibyl's sacred books, which have long since disappeared.

Baffling books

The Romans believed that when Rome began the gods spoke to a prophetess called the Cumaean Sibyl, giving her a set of prophesies (predictions) for its rulers to follow. These were written down in sacred books and kept in Rome's most important temple. The sibyl lived in a cave and sang out her prophesies or wrote them on oak leaves left at her cave entrance.

The geese of Juno (shown here in a Roman mosaic) became sacred animals for the Romans because they saved Rome.

Tough town

At first Rome was a rough and dangerous outlaws' town. There weren't many women and no one was keen to let their daughters marry the dodgy incomers. So, according to legend, the Romans invited the local Sabine tribe to a party – then kidnapped their women!

The Gauls attacked Rome in 390 BCE, and Roman forces retreated to the Capitoline Hill. In the dead of night the Gauls climbed the hill to take the Romans by surprise, but the sacred geese of Juno squawked loudly and raised the alarm, saving the Romans.

FIGHTING TO SURVIVE

In its early years Rome had to beat off some formidable enemies.

For many years Rome fought Carthage, a city on the shores of North Africa. When Roman forces finally conquered Carthage they destroyed it and covered its lands with salt so that nothing would ever grow there again.

Carthaginian General Hannibal nearly defeated Rome when he marched his army and his fighting elephants across the Alps and launched a surprise attack.

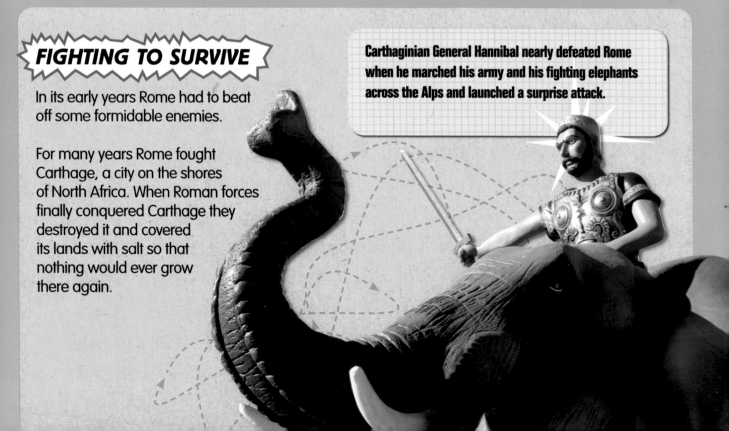

POSH PLOTTERS AND ROWDY REBELS

At first Rome had kings, but then it governed itself with a type of parliament called the Senate. This was meant to be a fair and efficient way to run things, except that bribery and murder got in the way…

Speech-making was very important at the Senate, and the best speech-makers became famous.

Fighting for power

At first senators only came from the oldest and wealthiest families in Rome, the Patricians. Gradually people from ordinary families, called Plebians, gained more power. Each year two consuls were elected to lead the Senate, often winning the contest through bribery.

ROME IN DANGER

In 63 BCE, a group of aristocrats planned to overthrow the Senate in a plot called the Catiline Conspiracy. When it was foiled, the plotters were sentenced to death and strangled.

In 73 BCE a group of slave gladiators escaped from a gladiator school. By the following year their group of rebels had grown to 120,000, led by a gladiator called Spartacus.

The Senate sent the army to fight the slaves, who were finally defeated after several battles. Spartacus probably died on the battlefield, but 6,000 of his followers were crucified along the road to Rome.

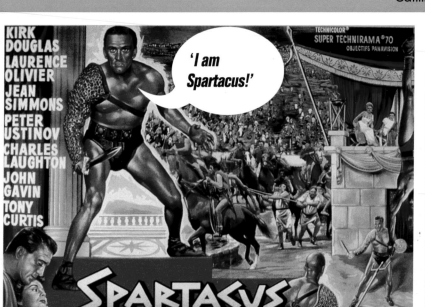

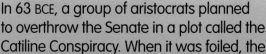

In 1960, the story of Spartacus became a famous Hollywood movie starring Kirk Douglas.

JULIUS CAESAR RULES OK

By 49 BCE the Senate was in chaos. Senators were having each other murdered and running violent street gangs. Finally a Patrician called Julius Caesar took power for himself. A group of senators murdered him in 44 BCE, but his family went on to become the first emperors of Rome.

Julius Caesar, probably the most famous Roman in the world.

TEN STRANGE BUT TRUE FACTS ABOUT JULIUS CAESAR

Caesar was kidnapped by pirates, made friends with them – and had them executed as soon as they freed him.

He had a son with Cleopatra, Queen of Egypt.

He hated being bald, so he wore a crown of laurel leaves.

He was handed a note warning him of his own murder, but he didn't read it.

He was the first Roman to be turned into a god.

He is thought to have suffered from either malaria or epilepsy.

He wrote history books and poems.

He changed the Latin name of the month Quintilis to Julius, now called July.

He changed the calendar to a fixed 365 days in a year.

His family claimed to be related to Venus, the Roman goddess of love.

Caesar's murder

Caesar was on his way to the Senate when he was repeatedly stabbed by a jostling crowd of senators. His murder led to civil war between leading Romans and eventually to victory for Caesar's great-nephew Octavian. Octavian became Augustus, Rome's first emperor.

DON'T ARGUE WITH THE ARMY

The secret of Rome's success was its highly-trained organised army, which conquered other lands and defended borders.

Conquered tribes had to pay a regular tax, called a Tribute, to Roman officials. The tax helped to pay for the army.

The army was not allowed to enter Rome itself, in case it caused trouble.

Soldiers were trained to march up to 30km (18 miles) a day.

Marching columns were sometimes so long that the front troops had started to pitch camp when the back troops had only just started to march.

Roman soldiers wore boots with iron hobnails in the soles, which made a loud noise.

Roman soldiers had to sign on for 25 years of service.

Roman soldiers lead captives in chains through Rome, in a Triumph parade.

Army asides

The army sent back treasure and slaves to Rome from the lands it conquered.

Whoever was in charge of the army at the time of a great victory might be allowed a Triumph, a grand parade through Rome to show off captured treasures, including prisoners-of-war.

As well as regular troops, Rome had secret agents called speculatores, whose job it was to infiltrate enemy forces and send back information.

Soldiers who broke the army's strict rules were punished. Troops found guilty of serious crimes could be beheaded, hanged, burnt alive or sent to fight in the arena.

Soldiers weren't allowed to marry until they retired, but they could have girlfriends and children. Their family might live in a shanty town called a vicus, outside their military base.

The Iceni, under their leader Boudica, massacred Roman veterans in Colchester.

THE BIG BULLY BOYS

The Praetorian Guard was the only group of soldiers allowed to work in Rome itself. They were the Emperor's crack bodyguards, but they regularly turned on their bosses, murdering them and putting new men in power. Eventually the Guard was disbanded in disgrace.

Emperors were rightly afraid of the Guard. After the Guard had stabbed Emperor Caligula to death, Claudius, whom they wanted to make emperor in his place, hid from them behind a curtain and had to be persuaded to come out.

DISASTER FOR THE VETS

Retired Roman soldiers were given land in conquered territories. In England this policy led to a terrible disaster for veterans settled in Camulodunum, now called Colchester. In 60 CE the local Iceni tribe, angered by ill-treatment, attacked and destroyed the town, killing veterans and their families barricaded inside the Temple of Claudius.

The Praetorian Guard wore a red-crested helmet and muscly-looking breastplate.

WHO'S UP AND WHO'S DOWN

Rome was a very snobbish place, and Romans had to be careful to wear the right clothes and behave in the right way, depending on their social rank. If they didn't do things properly, they risked disgrace.

A senator – a super-rich Roman bigshot.

Male senators were born into noble families and were expected to own property worth more than a million sesterces (now worth roughly US$ 3 million). They weren't allowed to make money from business or marry someone who was lower class.

A politician and soldier called Crassus was said to be the richest Roman ever. After his death in 53 BCE it is said that his enemies poured molten gold down his throat as a symbol of his thirst for money.

Each senator was the patron of a group of less important people called his clients. He was expected to help them in return for their loyalty.

During the day clients were expected to follow their patron around in a crowd to show everyone that he was a high-ranking person.

If a senator was elected to the official position of 'magistrate' he could have bodyguards who carried a bundle of rods and an axe.

Next in rank after senators were equestrians, businessmen worth 400,000 sesterces (roughly US$ 1,200,000 today).

An equestrian, a wealthy gentleman of ancient Rome.

Ordinary Roman plebeians out shopping at a knife store.

Re-enactors wearing togas with purple stripes, showing they were important Romans.

Next came the plebeians, ordinary Roman citizens who could only go up the social ladder if they got rich enough.

At the bottom of the social pile were slaves owned by their masters. Someone might be born a slave or be captured in battle.

Women were controlled by their fathers or husbands, and weren't allowed to take part in public life.

Wear the right thing

The mark of an important Roman was his toga, a 6-m (19-ft) long strip of woollen cloth wrapped around the body over a tunic. Senators wore togas with a broad purple stripe. Equestrians wore togas with a narrow stripe, and the very grandest Romans wore all-over purple togas at special events. Purple toga dye was made from the glandular fluid of sea snails, and was very expensive.

Feel sorry for the slaves

It's thought that by 200 CE nearly a third of all the people living in Rome were slaves. In fact, without slaves ancient Rome could never have been successful.

Slaves could be freed by their masters or save up and pay for their freedom. Freed slaves were called freedmen.

Professional slave-hunters tracked down escaped slaves, who were savagely punished.

Slaves did all the housework, cooking, cleaning and manual labour in ancient Rome.

13

MURDERERS AND MADMEN

SHOCKING CELEBRITY STORIES

Roman history is full of shocking stories about emperors and their families. Here is a small selection of the tales that have survived.

TRUTH WARNING

The gossip we have about Roman emperors comes from ancient historians who may have exaggerated or even made things up.

THE FAMILY FROM HELL?

In 27 BCE **Octavian** took power in Rome, changed his name to Augustus and became the first emperor. His relatives ruled for the next few generations, but they had a habit of killing each other to grab power. They had themselves declared gods when they died.

Tiberius (emperor from 14–37 CE) Family members he didn't like were starved to death or executed.

Claudius (41–54 CE) It is said that Claudius died after eating a plate of mushrooms poisoned by his fourth wife, who was later killed by her own son, Nero.

Caligula (37–41 CE) Caligula was obsessed with his horse and planned to make it head of the Senate. He married his sister and had many people cruelly murdered before he himself was assassinated.

Nero (54–68 CE) He tried to drown his mother before having her stabbed. He was eventually overthrown and was condemned to be flogged to death but killed himself before he was captured.

Commodus (centre) liked to fight as a gladiator, but nobody was allowed to beat him.

DEAD AWFUL

Emperors died by stoning, stabbing, strangling, poisoning and beheading. Here are just a few examples:

Commodus (180–192 CE) liked to fight as a gladiator, and especially enjoyed killing defenceless animals, such as giraffes. His enemies fed him poison, but he survived by throwing it all up. Finally the Senate sent his favourite wrestler to strangle him in the bath.

The Emperor Elagabalus dressed as a woman and worshipped the Sun.

Caracalla (211–217 CE) had his brother and sister-in-law killed. Then, when a play criticising him was performed in the city of Alexandria, he had the city burnt and looted. He was murdered by his bodyguards as he was taking a pee by the side of the road.

Elagabalus (218–222 CE) was 14 when he became emperor. He offered a fortune to any doctor willing to turn him into a woman. In the end, he never got the chance because his bodyguards had other plans. They dragged him from his hiding place in a public toilet and killed him, along with his mother.

A dangerous job

Some emperors inherited the title, some took it by force, and one even bought it in an auction. Sometimes there were four, five or even six different emperors in a year.

BIRTHS, MARRIAGES AND DEATHS

Roman families had traditional customs and ceremonies, just as families do today.

Tiny pottery toys for a Roman child.

Baby Romans

In Roman families the oldest male was in charge, and nobody could do anything without his agreement. When a child was born it was placed at the feet of its father. If the father picked it up, it was accepted into the family; if not, it could be left outside to die.

Roman children had toys such as clay and wax dolls, yo-yos, spinning tops, balls and stilts. All children had a lucky locket called a bulla.

When boys reached maturity, at about 14, they started to wear a toga. They were registered as a Roman citizen, and the family celebrated with a dinner.

Boys from well-off families were taught reading, writing, maths and Greek by tutors or in small schools. Girls rarely got any education, but were taught domestic jobs such as spinning.

The Emperor Nero as a young boy, wearing his bulla (lucky locket).

NAME THAT ROMAN

Important Romans had three names – a personal name, the name of their family clan, then the name of their clan branch. For instance, Julius Caesar's name was Gaius Julius Caesar. His family would have called him Gaius and his friends would have called him Caesar.

A fresco (wall painting) of a young married couple, found at Pompeii.

Let's get married!

Roman marriages were organised by parents, who chose brides and grooms for their children.

The bride wore a flame-coloured veil over a long white tunic. She wore a wreath of flowers on her head.

She wore a wedding ring on the third finger of her left hand, because Romans thought this finger was connected to the heart.

The couple made vows in front of witnesses and then there was a feast. The priest offered some cake to the god Jupiter before it was shared between the guests.

After the ceremony the bride left her house to go to her new home, followed by a noisy procession of her family and friends. Musicians played and people threw nuts.

Divorce became quite common in Rome. Sometimes fathers ordered their daughters to divorce their husbands, in order to marry someone more useful to the family.

OFF TO THE AFTERLIFE

When Romans died, their relatives put a coin in their mouth to pay the ferryman Charon, who was said to row dead souls across a lake to the underworld, where the dead lived. The body would usually be cremated and put in an urn in a tomb outside the city of Rome.

The remains of a Roman tomb, found outside the city

THE EMPIRE INDOORS

The type of home a Roman lived in depended on how wealthy and important they were.

The grand London palace of the Roman Governor of Britain, around 80 CE.

Best and worst addresses

Well-to-do Romans were very snobbish. They looked down on people who lived in the wrong part of town.

Emperors lived in beautifully furnished mansions. Nero lived in the enormous Golden Palace, its walls decorated with gold leaf, gemstones and rare seashells.

Wealthy Romans had big holiday homes on the coast. The grandest ones had large fishponds.

Well-off Roman city-dwellers lived in a single-storey house (villa) called a domus, in one of the smart districts.

The Roman poor lived in crowded slums in the swampiest, most unhealthy districts of the city.

DOWN IN THE SLUMS

Poor people lived in multi-storey apartment blocks called insulae. These were so badly built that they often collapsed. There were five or six floors, but no toilets or kitchens.

People threw their rubbish out into the streets, including the contents of their toilet pots. This was illegal but the law was only enforced in the daytime so people tended to do it at night.

ROUND THE VILLA

Smart Roman townhouses had rooms built around two courtyards, decorated with fountains and outdoor marble seats.

Some homes had a model phallus (penis) with tiny wings hanging above the front door, as a symbol of good luck.

...ublic rooms such as dining rooms were grand.

Every house had its own ...ivate altar, the lararium, for ...rshipping household spirits called lares.

Houses faced inwards, with no windows out onto the street.

There was good plumbing, and villas had fresh running water.

Bedrooms were often cramped and stuffy.

RUDE WRITINGS

Some Romans wrote rude Latin graffiti on buildings. Here are some translations of examples from the ancient town of Pompeii:

Oppius is a clown, a thief and a crook!

LUCIUS PAINTED THIS!

To the one who keeps pooing here. Beware of the curse. If you look down on this curse, may you have angry Jupiter for an enemy.

Five Roman home truths

Romans kept dogs, caged birds and ferrets as pets, but cats were rare.

One wealthy Roman girl kept an eel as a pet in her fishpond, and fitted it with gold earrings.

Romans wore slippers indoors.

There were spoons and knives but no forks in

LOOKING GOOD, LATIN-STYLE

Being clean and smart was very important to the Romans.

Bathhouse remains in Bath (Aquae Sulis) where the Romans bathed in hot springs.

Rules of the pool

Romans visited public bathhouses (baths) every day. There were sets of rooms with hot and cold plunge pools, a swimming pool and rooms for exercising or relaxing. The baths were like clubs where the 'in-crowd' met to hear the latest gossip.

In Rome there were giant public baths that even had libraries and theatres attached to them. One could hold up to 3,000 bathers.

As well as bathing, Romans exercised at the baths – playing ball games, racket games or lifting weights. They could also get a massage, have their body hair plucked, gamble, play board games or buy snacks.

The public baths were a place for wannabe performers to get noticed. Poets, musicians, acrobats and jugglers turned up, hoping to get party bookings.

An olive oil bottle and a strigil for skin-scraping.

Romans didn't use soap. Their bath slaves rubbed olive oil on them and then scraped it off with a metal scraper called a strigil. The dirt came off with the oil.

GOTTA GO

Roman towns had public toilets, a line of holes cut into a bench over a channel of running water. Romans could chat together, then wipe their bottoms using sea sponges fixed to sticks.

Fullers were textile workers who helped make woollen cloth, and they needed urine to use in their work. They put pots outside their workshops for anyone to pee in as they walked by.

Emperor Vespasian imposed a tax on urine gathered from public toilets by the fullers, and accidentally connected his name to toilets forever. In modern Italy men's public urinals are still called *vespasiani*.

Pass the sponge, please! A row of Roman public toilets – where you got to know your neighbours really well.

Top Roman beauty tips

Here are some of the make-up tricks and treatments the Romans used.

The sweat of top Roman gladiators was thought to improve the skin. Pots of it were sold to female fans.

Cheeks were reddened with rouge made from rose petals, powdered lead or even crocodile dung.

Roman make-up and face creams were made from all kinds of ingredients, some of them very smelly, including calf urine and sheep sweat.

Pure white skin was prized, so women wore pale skin make-up made from dangerous powdered lead, which eventually damaged the skin badly.

Roman toothpaste was made from powdery pumice stone ground with salt.

Make-up slaves mixed up potions and lotions for their mistresses, often spitting into the mixture to help mix it.

21

FISH PORRIDGE, ANYONE?

FOOD FIT FOR AN EMPIRE

What could you expect to eat if you took a time machine back to ancient Rome? After reading this, you might want to pack your own picnic…

Smelly sauce

The Romans loved a fish sauce called garum, which they stored in pottery jars and mixed into all sorts of food.

How to make garum

1. Collect some fish guts. Mix the stinky slop with some salt and leave it to bubble up in the Sun.

2. Strain the fishy liquid that runs out of the fish guts as it ferments. Store it in jars and use it in every recipe you can.

3. Give the leftover fish bits and pieces to poor people or slaves to eat in their porridge.

Customers could sit at street bars to enjoy a drink or a snack.

ROMAN TAKEAWAYS

Cauponas were street counters where you could buy a drink and a snack. But if you did this, you'd be showing yourself up. Cauponas were for poor people and the bar owners were viewed as scum.

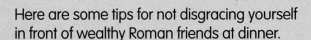

MANNERS, PLEASE

Here are some tips for not disgracing yourself in front of wealthy Roman friends at dinner.

Don't ask for brown bread. It was considered peasant food.

Don't eat standing up. Wealthy Romans ate lying down.

Don't ask for butter. Butter wasn't eaten. It was rubbed onto wounds.

Don't ask for more meat. Romans didn't eat much meat, and criticised foreigners for their meat-eating habits.

Dinners to die for

Only the very wealthiest Roman aristocrats went to banquets. These were spectacular expensive occasions. Meals took up to eight hours, and guests peed in vases provided by slaves, rather than get up to leave the room.

Important Romans had to be careful what they ate. Professional poisoners could be hired to kill enemies, but people could employ food tasters to test out food for poison.

Examples of banquet dishes included:

Ostrich brains eaten from the bird's head.

Roast pig stuffed with live birds that flew out when the meat was cut.

Goatfish allowed to die at the table because it turned a pretty colour.

Camels' feet

DINE WITH THE EMPEROR

The Emperor Elagabalus liked to have a joke with his banquet guests. He put out whoopee cushions for them to sit on and once let some lions loose in the dining room.

The Emperor Hadrian's favourite food was a meat pasty.

The Emperor Tiberius loved vegetables, especially cucumbers and cabbage. He got angry with relatives who refused to eat their greens!

Slaves kept guests supplied with wine and food, while performers entertained them.

BE NICE TO THE GODS, OR ELSE!

Romans worshipped many gods and goddesses and worked hard to keep them happy.

FIVE TOP GODS

KNOW YOUR GODS

Each Roman god specialised in a different aspect of life, and Romans chose which ones to pray to.

The gods could send signals to mortals via omens, signs such as birds flying overhead or an eclipse of the Sun. Priests were trained to interpret the omens and decide if they were good or bad.

The big boss: Jupiter was the king of the gods. He could hurl thunderbolts from the sky if he was angry.

Good time god: Bacchus was the god of wine and partying.

Tricky lady: Juno was Jupiter's wife and also his sister. She was easy to upset, and could arrange the death of anyone who displeased her.

Holy at home: Vesta was the goddess of the home and hearth (fireplace). In her temple in Rome a fire was kept alight, tended by six important priestesses called Vestal Virgins.

Please please me

The best way to please the gods was to offer sacrifices. Priests killed animals on official altars at public ceremonies and said the correct prayers. But if a priest got the words wrong, the whole ceremony had to start again.

In times of national crisis, lots of animals were sacrificed in one long ceremony, to get the gods on Rome's side. But if the gods were judged to have failed to keep their side of a bargain, ceremonies to honour them were cancelled.

Priests were trained to read the auspices – to study the entrails (innards) of sacrificed animals, especially the liver, to get signs from the gods.

The inside of the Temple of Mithras, or Mithraeum, in Rome.

Hot temper: Vulcan was the blacksmith of the gods. It was thought that if he stoked his fires too much or got angry, volcano Mount Vesuvius (shown in the distance, above) would erupt.

TEMPLE SECRETS

Roman soldiers had their own secret religious cult – the worship of sun god Mithras. New members of the cult had to stand in a pit to be drenched with blood from a bull sacrificed above them.

Temples were dark places full of burning incense and giant statues of the gods. Sometimes people claimed to see these statues move, sweat or bleed.

25

MIND THE BLOOD

The Romans liked lively entertainment. They enjoyed bloodthirsty gladiator fights and rude theatre plays.

Death matches

At the end of a fight the crowd could decide if a defeated gladiator should be killed or spared because he fought well. They shouted "Iugula!" (Kill him!) or "Mitte!" (Let him go!) and signalled what they wanted with their thumb.

Occasionally there were women gladiatrixes, too. They fought bare-chested and without helmets. The Emperor Domitian is said to have staged torch-lit fights between women and dwarves.

A man dressed as a demon came into the arena at the end of a fight and dragged the dead bodies away, finishing off badly-injured gladiators with a hammer.

Fights to the death between gladiators were staged in giant arenas around the Empire. The biggest arena was the Colosseum in Rome (right), which could seat 50,000 people.

Gladiators had no choice whether to fight or not because they were slaves or prisoners. But if a gladiator became a star fighter, surviving many fights, he could become very rich and win his freedom.

THEATRE THINGS

The Romans loved plays, which were performed in open-air theatres. They were either tragedies full of death and murder, or rude comedies with lots of funny mix-ups and dirty jokes.

If the crowd really liked the play they would flap the corners of their togas in the air. If they didn't like it, they might start to throw things at the actors!

If a play script called for someone to die onstage, a condemned criminal was occasionally brought on, to be executed for real.

Romans liked music, too. The Roman writer Juvenal complained about silly Roman women fan-worshipping famous singers and stealing souvenirs of their performances.

Wealthy Romans paid for the plays to be put on, to make themselves popular and intellectual-looking. Sometimes they also paid members of the crowd to clap and cheer.

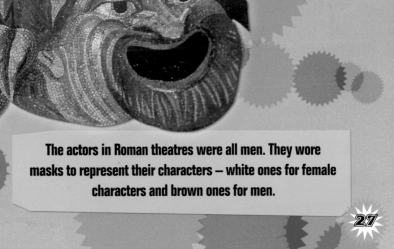

The actors in Roman theatres were all men. They wore masks to represent their characters – white ones for female characters and brown ones for men.

CELEBRATE ROMAN-STYLE

Romans loved parties, and had festivals of one sort or another throughout the year.

Year-round events

Here are just a few of the many events held through the year. Some of them sound very weird!

FEBRUARY 13TH TO 15TH: LUPERCALIA

This very ancient festival was a sort of spiritual spring-cleaning to avert evil spirits and purify Rome. Lupercus was the god of shepherds and his priests wore goatskins. Here's how Roman writer Plutarch described the goings-on:

'Noble youths run through the city naked, for sport and laughter striking those they meet with shaggy thongs.'

People deliberately got in the way, believing it was lucky to be hit with the animal-skin whips.

MARCH AND OCTOBER: BACCHANALIA

Wild parties were held, dedicated to the god Bacchus (also called Dionysus). These became so scandalous and out-of-control that the Senate banned them, on pain of death.

FEBRUARY 21ST: FERALIA

Families would picnic at the tombs of their dead relatives. They poured libations (offerings of wine) on the tombs for their ancestors.

MAY 1ST AND DECEMBER: BONA DEA

These festivals were for women only. The winter one was a private party held at the house of an important Roman lady. All men, male animals and even pictures of men had to be removed from the building, and any man seeing the evening's secret religious rites risked the punishment of blinding.

A miracle flame appears, sent by the gods, during a Bona Dea women-only ceremony.

AUGUST 21ST: CONSUALIA

Working animals such as horses and oxen were given a holiday and garlands of flowers were hung around their neck.

END OF DECEMBER: SATURNALIA

A week-long holiday for everyone, to celebrate the god Saturn, father of Jupiter. Everybody gave gifts and there were special markets. For once, slaves were served a banquet by their masters.

Fun and games

During the year there were various Roman games held to celebrate the gods, with markets, sport and theatrical performances. These included the Ludi Florales, a festival of fertility equivalent to May Day, still celebrated in parts of the world today. The games were held in the Circus Maximus, a large outdoor arena and racetrack in Rome.

ROMAN DATE RECYCLING

When the Christian Church was set up in the 400s a number of the ancient Roman festival dates became times of Christian celebration. Saturnalia became Christmas, for instance. Early church leaders probably thought it would be easier for pagans to accept Christianity if some of their traditional days were used in the new religion.

An artist's impression of drunken Romans partying during Saturnalia, now celebrated as Christmas.

Augustus: The first Roman Emperor.

Auspices: Signs sent by the gods, in the innards of an animal.

Bacchus: Roman god of wine and parties.

Barbarians: The name given to people who lived outside the borders of the Roman Empire.

Byzantium: A city that became the centre of Roman rule. It was renamed Constantinople and is now called Istanbul.

Camulodunum: The name of Colchester in Roman times.

Capitoline Hill: One of the seven hills upon which the city of Rome was built.

Carthage: North African city that fought Rome until its forces were defeated and it was destroyed.

Caupona: A Roman street bar.

Charon: The mythical ferryman who took dead souls to the underworld.

Citizen: Someone with the right to call themselves Roman. Roman citizens had legal rights that others did not have.

Cleopatra: Queen of Egypt, who tried to keep her country independent from Rome but failed.

Client: A person of lesser importance who was connected to an important Roman patron, and was obliged to help them in return for favours.

Colosseum: A giant arena built in Rome, for gladiator shows.

Constantine: The first Christian Emperor of the Roman Empire.

Consul: Elected leader of the Roman Senate, rather like a prime minister.

Cult: A group that worships a god or goddess.

Domus: A luxury villa.

Emperor: Unelected ruler of Rome who passed rule down through his family.

Freedman: A slave who was now officially free.

Fresco: Decorative wall painting.

Garum: A sauce made from fermented fish guts.

Gauls: People from the areas we now call France, Belgium, western Germany and northern Italy.

Gladiator: A trained fighter, usually a slave or captured prisoner-of-war, who fought to the death in a public show.

Gladiatrix: A trained female gladiator who fought in shows.

Goths: The name given to tribes originating in areas we now call Germany, Russia and Scandinavia.

Hannibal: Carthaginian general who fought Rome and very nearly won.

Insulae: Roman multi-storey apartment blocks.

Juno: The most important Roman goddess, the wife of Jupiter, King of the Gods.

Jupiter: King of the Roman gods.

Lararium: A private household altar.

Lares: Household spirits, who were thought to watch over families and homes.

Libation: A ceremonial pouring of wine as an offering to the gods and goddesses.

Ludi: Official Roman games, held over a few days or weeks.

Mars: Roman god of war.

Mithras: A sun god worshipped by Roman soldiers.

Mount Vesuvius: An active volcano in southern Italy.

Omen: A sign sent by the gods and goddesses.

Oration: The art of speech-making. Skilful orators were highly praised in Rome.

Pagans: People who worship gods and goddesses, not the god of the Christian faith.

Patrician: Someone from one of Rome's old aristocratic families.

Patron: An important Roman who was connected to people of lesser importance, who he was obliged to help if he could.

Phallus: A penis-shaped object, regarded as lucky by the Romans.

Plebian: An ordinary Roman, with no special rank in society.

Praetorian Guard: The Roman Emperor's bodyguard.

Prophesies: Predictions of the future sent by the gods.

Relics: Objects said to be directly connected to religious events or people.

Sacred geese of Juno: A flock of geese kept at a sacred temple on Capitoline Hill in Rome.

Sacrifice: The ceremonial killing of an animal, as a gift for gods and goddesses.

Saturnalia: An important Roman festival held at the end of December.

Senate: A type of parliament that made Roman laws.

Senator: A member of the ruling class that made the laws of Rome.

Sesterce: A Roman coin.

Slave: Someone with no rights, owned by their master.

Spartacus: A gladiator who led a band of escaped slaves against Rome, but was defeated.

Strigil: A tool for scraping olive oil off the skin.

Toga: A piece of clothing worn by Roman men – a length of woollen cloth that could be wrapped around the body over a tunic.

Tribe: A group of people linked by customs and language, living together and ruled by one or more leaders.

Underworld: The place where Romans believed that the souls of the dead went.

Vandals: A tribe who settled in North Africa and then attacked Rome.

Venus: Roman goddess of love and beauty.

Vesta: Roman goddess of the home and hearth (fireplace).

Vestal Virgins: Important Roman priestesses who looked after the Temple of Vesta in Rome.

Veterans: Old soldiers.

Vicus: A shanty town outside a Roman military fort.

Vulcan: A god who made volcanoes erupt.

ROMAN WEBSITES

http://www.bbc.co.uk/history/ancient/romans/
Lots of information on what the Roman Empire was really like.

www.britishmuseum.org/explore/highlights/highlights_search_results.aspx?RelatedId=1810
See hundreds of Roman objects found in different parts of the Empire.

http://www.pbs.org/wgbh/nova/lostempires/roman/
Wander through a reconstructed Roman baths, build a Roman aqueduct and try out some Roman recipes.

http://besthistorysites.net/index.php/ancient-biblical-history/rome
A list of good Roman websites.

Note to parents and teachers

Every effort has been made by the Publishers to ensure that the websites in this book are suitable for children, that they are of the highest educational value, and that they contain no inappropriate or offensive material. However, because of the nature of the Internet, it is impossible to guarantee that the contents of these sites will not be altered. We strongly advise that Internet access is supervised by a responsible adult.

actors 27
afterlife 17
army 8, 10–11
Augustus, Emperor 9, 14

banquets 23, 29
bathhouse/baths 20
Boudica 11

Caesar, Julius 9, 16
Caligula, Emperor 11, 14
Caracalla, Emperor 15
Carthage 7
Catiline Conspiracy 8
cauponas 22
children 16
Claudius, Emperor 11, 14
cleanliness 20
Colchester 11
Colosseum 26
Commodus, Emperor 15
Crassus 12
Cumaean Sibyl 6

education 16
Elagabalus, Emperor 15, 23
equestrians 12, 13

family life 16–17
festivals 28–29
food 22–23

garam 22
Gauls 7
gladiators/gladiatrixes 8, 15, 21, 26

gods, Roman 6, 9, 14, 24–25, 28, 29
  Bacchus 24, 28
  Juno 7, 24
  Jupiter 17, 19, 24, 29
  Lupercus 28
  Mars 6
  Mithras 25
  Saturn 29
  Venus 9
  Vesta 24
  Vulcan 25
graffiti 19

Hadrian, Emperor 23
Hannibal, General 7
houses 18–19

Iceni 11
insulae 18

Juvenal 27

make-up 21
manners, table 22
marriage 17

names 16
Nero, Emperor 14, 16

Octavian (see also Augustus) 9, 14

Patricians 8, 9
Plebians 8, 13, 23
Plutarch 28
Praetorian Guard 11
Pompeii 17, 19, 23

priests/priestesses 24, 25
prophesies 6

religion 24–25, 28, 29
Remus 6
Rome 6, 7, 8, 9, 10, 11, 13, 14, 17, 20, 24, 25, 26, 28
Romulus 6

sacrifices 25
Senate, the 8, 9, 14, 15, 28
senators 8, 9, 12, 13
slaves 8, 10, 13, 21, 22, 23, 26, 29
soldiers 10, 11, 25
Spartacus 8

temples 6, 11, 24–25
theatres 20, 26, 27
Tiberius, Emperor 14, 23
togas 13, 16, 27
toilets 15, 21
toys 16
Triumph, a 10

Vespasian, Emperor 21
villas 18, 19